Law and Crime

Level 6 – Orange

Helpful Hints for Reading at Home

The graphemes (written letters) and phonemes (units of sound) used throughout this series are aligned with Letters and Sounds. This offers a consistent approach to learning, whether reading at home or in the classroom.

HERE IS A LIST OF PHONEMES FOR THIS PHASE OF LEARNING. AN EXAMPLE OF THE PRONUNCIATION CAN BE FOUND IN BRACKETS.

Phase 5			
ay (day)	ou (out)	ie (tie)	ea (eat)
oy (boy)	ir (girl)	ue (blue)	aw (saw)
wh (when)	ph (photo)	ew (new)	oe (toe)
au (Paul)	a_e (make)	e_e (these)	i_e (like)
o_e (home)	u_e (rule, cube)		

Phase 5 Alternative Pronunciations of Graphemes			
a (hat, what)	e (bed, she)	i (fin, find)	o (hot, so, other)
u (but, unit)	c (cat, cent)	g (got, giant)	ow (cow, blow)
ie (tied, field)	ea (eat, bread)	er (farmer, herb)	ch (chin, school, chef)
y (yes, by, very)	ou (out, shoulder, could, you)		

HERE ARE SOME WORDS WHICH YOUR CHILD MAY FIND TRICKY.

Phase 5 Tricky Words			
oh	their	people	Mr
Mrs	looked	called	asked
could			

TOP TIPS FOR HELPING YOUR CHILD TO READ:

- Allow children time to break down unfamiliar words into units of sound and then encourage children to string these sounds together to create the word.

- Encourage your child to point out any focus phonics when they are used.

- Read through the book more than once to grow confidence.

- Ask simple questions about the text to assess understanding.

- Encourage children to use illustrations as prompts.

This book focuses on /i_e/ and /igh/ and is an Orange level 6 book band.

Can you fill in the gaps?

bi_e

pi_e

vi_e

sli_e

Answers: bike, pipe, vine, slime

All people have to stick to the law. Laws tell people what they can and cannot do. We say that a person has committed a crime when they do something that is not allowed under the law.

Crime can hurt the people who do it. It can hurt the people around them, too. We have laws to protect people.

Stealing is a crime. It is bad to go out of a shop without paying for the things that you have got.

Fighting is a crime unless you are doing a fighting sport, such as boxing. People who fight as a sport still have to keep to the laws to keep people from getting hurt.

Boxer

To drive, you must do a test about traffic laws. When you finish, you will get a card that says you are allowed to drive.

Trespassing is the name given to the crime of being at a spot you are not allowed to be at. Do not trespass on a site if a person tells you that you cannot be there.

People who commit crimes are criminals. If they hide from the law, people will come looking for them so they can arrest them.

Criminal

A criminal will have a hard time getting out of handcuffs. They are locked on tight so that the suspect cannot slide out.

Handcuffs

For lesser crimes, criminals might get a fine. For bigger crimes, they may have to go to jail for a long time.

Some criminals might spend a few years in jail. Some might end up spending all their lives there. They can never go out.

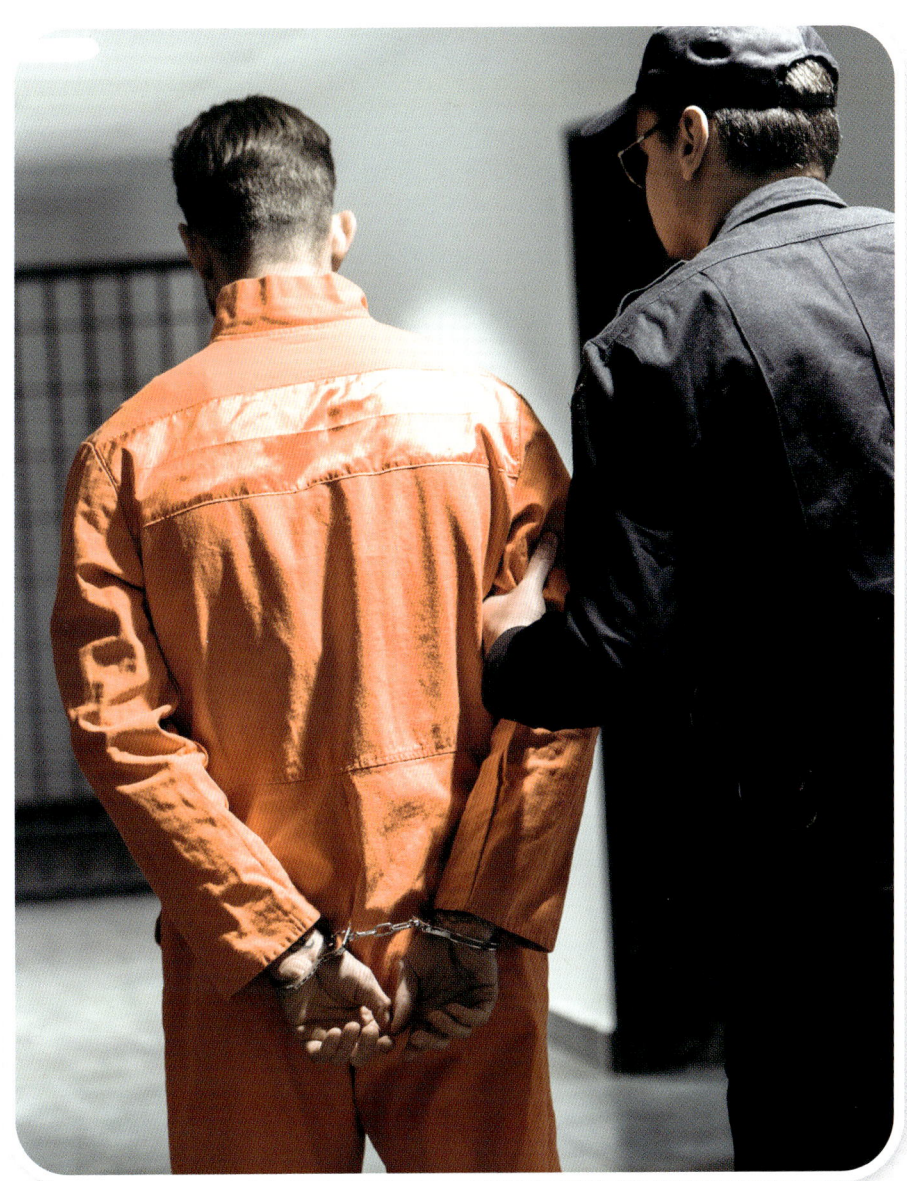

What can you do if you see a crime? If you are in the UK, you can ring nine nine nine to get help.

Not all people can ring nine nine nine.
You might have to ring a different number.
Ask an adult to tell you the right number.

©2023 **BookLife Publishing Ltd.**
King's Lynn, Norfolk, PE30 4LS, UK

ISBN 978-1-80505-081-0

All rights reserved. Printed in China.
A catalogue record for this book is
available from the British Library.

Law and Crime
Written by Charis Mather
Designed by Lucy Otter

An Introduction to BookLife Readers...

Our Readers have been specifically created in line with the London Institute of Education's approach to book banding and are phonetically decodable and ordered to support each phase of the Letters and Sounds document.

Each book has been created to provide the best possible reading and learning experience. Our aim is to share our love of books with children, providing both emerging readers and prolific page-turners with beautiful books that are guaranteed to provoke interest and learning, regardless of ability.

BOOK BAND GRADED using the Institute of Education's approach to levelling.

PHONETICALLY DECODABLE supporting each phase of Letters and Sounds.

EXERCISES AND QUESTIONS to offer reinforcement and to ascertain comprehension.

CLEAR DESIGN to inspire and provoke engagement, providing the reader with clear visual representations of each non-fiction topic.

AUTHOR INSIGHT:
CHARIS MATHER

Charis Mather is a children's author at BookLife Publishing who has a love for reading and writing. Her studies in linguistics and experiences working with young readers have given her a knack for writing material that suits a range of ages and skill levels. Charis is passionate about producing books that emphasise the fun in reading and is convinced that no matter how much you already know, there is always something new to learn.

This book focuses on /i_e/ and /igh/ and is an Orange level 6 book band.

Image Credits Images are courtesy of Shutterstock.com. With thanks to Getty Images, Thinkstock Photo and iStockphoto. Cover – Anatolir, Meilun, OSTILL is Franck Camhi, teh_z1b, Yuliia Konakhovska. 2–3 – MossStudio, Creatus, Nature Design, New Africa. 4–5 – Ground Picture, Powerofflowers. 6–7 – Lucky Business, Mike_shots. 8–9 – Larisa Rudenko, Vitalii Stock. 10–11 – Brian Minkoff, Julian Popov. 12–13 – JaneHYork, LightField Studios. 14–15 – Simon Vayro, vystekimages.